Start with Art

Photographs

Isabel Thomas

www.raintreepublishers.co.uk
Visit our website to find out more information about Raintree books.

To order:
☎ Phone 0845 6044371
🖷 Fax +44 (0) 1865 312263
🖳 Email myorders@raintreepublishers.co.uk

Customers from outside the UK please telephone +44 1865 312262

Raintree is an imprint of Capstone Global Library Limited, a company incorporated in England and Wales having its registered office at 7 Pilgrim Street, London, EC4V 6LB – Registered company number: 6695582

Edited by Dan Nunn, Rebecca Rissman, and Catherine Veitch
Designed by Richard Parker
Picture research by Mica Brancic and Hannah Taylor
Originated by Capstone Global Library
Printed and bound in China by South China Printing Company Ltd

ISBN 978 1 406 22411 5
15 14 13 12 11
10 9 8 7 6 5 4 3 2 1

British Library Cataloguing in Publication Data
Thomas, Isabel
Photographs. -- (Start with art)
770-dc22
A full catalogue record for this book is available from the British Library.

Acknowledgements
We would like to thank the following for permission to reproduce photographs: Alamy Images p. 6 (© John Warburton-Lee Photography); Alexander Turnbull Library pp. 18, 23 – posed; © Capstone Global Library Ltd p. 7 (Lord & Leverett); © Capstone Publishers pp. 9, 20, 21, 22, 23 – digital camera (Karon Dubke); Corbis pp. 10 (Liu Dawei/xh/Xinhua Press), 12 (Reuters/Gary Hershorn), 16 (Charles Jones/© Sean Sexton Collection), 17 (Ansel Adams Publishing Rights Trust); Getty Images p. 4, 8 (Science & Society Picture Library/Royal Photographic Society); James Mollison p. 15; Robbie Cooper p. 11; Saatchi Gallery p. 19; Shutterstock pp. 5, 23 – background (© Hal_P), 13 (© iwka), 14, 23 – frame (© ellakay), 23 – gallery (© Shamleen), 23 – subject (© Nastenok), 23 – texture (© Konstantin Sutyagin).

Front cover photograph of Yosemite Valley, California, USA reproduced with permission of Corbis (© Ansel Adams Publishing Rights Trust). Back cover photograph of a child photographing tulips reproduced with permission of Shutterstock (© Hal_P). Back cover photograph of a digital camera reproduced with permission of © Capstone Publishers (Karon Dubke).

Every effort has been made to contact copyright holders of material reproduced in this book. Any omissions will be rectified in subsequent printings if notice is given to the publisher.

All the Internet addresses (URLs) given in this book were valid at the time of going to press. However, due to the dynamic nature of the Internet, some addresses may have changed, or sites may have changed or ceased to exist since publication. While the author and publisher regret any inconvenience this may cause readers, no responsibility for any such changes can be accepted by either the author or the publisher.

Contents

Some words are shown in bold, **like this**. You can find out what they mean by looking in the glossary.

What is a photograph?

A photograph is a picture taken with a camera.

This photograph of a hippopotamus was taken 160 years ago.

A person who takes photographs is called a photographer.

Anyone with a camera can be a photographer.

Where can I see photographs?

Museums and **galleries** display photographs for everyone to see.

Some photographers are very famous.

You can see photographs every day.

Find them in books, newspapers, magazines, and on the Internet.

What do people use to take photographs?

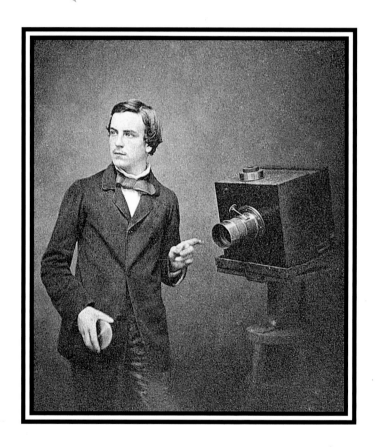

A camera is a machine that takes photographs.

The first cameras were big and heavy.

Now most people use **digital cameras**.

You can look at digital photographs on a computer or print them out.

Why do people take photographs?

Photographs can record people, places, and events.

They help us to remember the past.

Some artists take photographs instead of drawing or painting.

They can show us how the **subject** is feeling.

What can photographs show?

People like to take photographs of special events, beautiful places, and famous people.

These pictures show us what happens in other places.

Many artists take photographs of normal life.

They show that there are interesting things all around.

How do people take photographs?

Photographers **frame** their pictures carefully.

They take pictures from up high and down low.

They decide whether to get up close or stand far away.

They zoom in to show us details, or zoom out to show us the **background**.

How do photographers use light and dark?

light area

Good photographs have light areas and dark areas.

Light makes these vegetables look beautiful.

Many photographers take black and white photographs.

This can help the picture to show different **textures**.

What is a portrait?

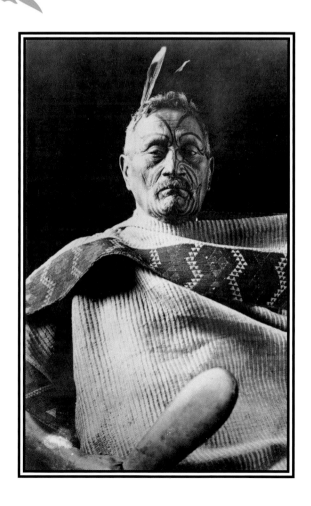

A portrait is a picture of a person.

This portrait is **posed**. The person knows he is being photographed.

This portrait is not posed.

What do the clothes, objects, and **background** tell you about the woman in this photograph?

Start to take photographs!

The photographers on pages 14 and 15 took good pictures by standing in different places.

1. Try taking photographs of a toy that you play with every day.

2. Take photographs from up high and down low.

3. Try standing above your **subject**. Then try standing below.

4. Try to take a few pictures that are different from each other.

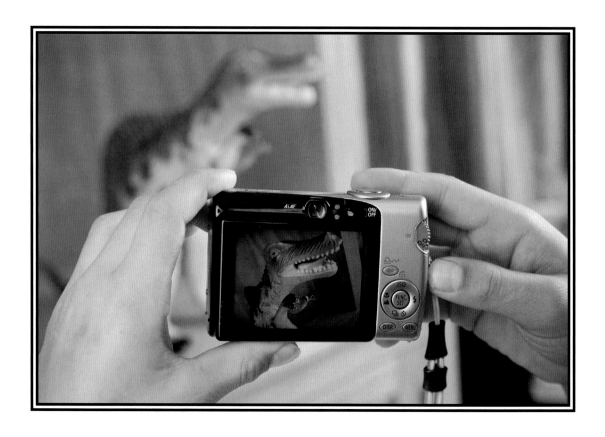

5. Look at the pictures on your camera. Are you happy with them? Do you want to take any more?

6. Print out your best pictures and make a classroom display.

Glossary

background things that are behind the main subject of a photograph, drawing, or painting

digital camera camera that takes and stores photographs so they can be opened on a computer

frame decide what will be in a photograph

gallery place where art is displayed for people to look at

posed set up by the photographer, who gives people instructions

subject person, place, or object shown in a piece of art

texture how the surface of something looks and feels

Find out more

Book
What is Art: What is Photography?, Karen Hosack
(Raintree, 2008)

Websites
On this website you can look at photographs taken by artists:
www.artsmia.org/index.php?section_id=120

Learn how to take great digital photographs on this website:
www.nga.gov/kids/zone/index.htm#photoop

Get tips and enter your best pictures in a competition on this
website: www.youngphotographeroftheyear.com

Index